National Data Collection on Police Use of Force

Jointly published with the
National Institute of Justice

Tom McEwen
*Institute for Law and Justice
Alexandria, Virginia*

April 1996, NCJ-160113

U.S. Department of Justice
Office of Justice Programs

Bureau of Justice Statistics
Jan Chaiken, Ph.D.
Director

National Institute of Justice
Jeremy Travis, J.D.
Director

This document was prepared under contract OJP-94-C-008 with support provided by the National Institute of Justice (NIJ) and Bureau of Justice Statistics (BJS), Office of Justice Programs, U.S. Department of Justice.

The points of view or opinions expressed in this document are those of the author and do not necessarily represent the official position or policies of the U.S. Department of Justice.

The author may be contacted at —

Institute for Law and Justice
1018 Duke Street
Alexandria, VA 22314

Phone: 703-684-5300
Fax: 703-739-5533

National Data Collection on Police Use of Force

The author would like to thank several people who reviewed drafts of this discussion paper. In addition to staff members at NIJ and BJS, beneficial comments were provided by Geoff Alpert, Professor, University of South Carolina; Edward F. Connors, President, Institute for Law and Justice (ILJ); Lorie Fridell, Professor, Florida State University; William A. Geller, Associate Director, Police Executive Research Forum; Joel Garner, Director of Research, Joint Centers for Justice Studies, Inc.; Robert Langworthy, Professor, University of Cincinnati; Neal Miller, Principal Associate, ILJ. Joan Peterschmidt on the ILJ staff provided excellent support in the preparation of the paper.

The text was improved considerably by the editing of Peter Ohlhausen of Alexandria, Virginia.

Yvonne Boston and Tom Hester of BJS proofread the final report, with Ms. Boston producing the camera copy under the supervision of Marilyn Marbrook.

Contents

Foreword

Introduction   1

Police Use of Force Workshop   5

Federal responses   10
    National data collection efforts   10
    Annual summaries   11
    Research on police use of force   13

Police use of force: An overview   16
    Prior studies of use of force   16
    Data reporting needs and police liability   24
    Consumers of police use of force data   27

Recent studies on police use of force   31
    National survey of police use of force   32
    State survey of police use of force   36
    Local survey of police use of force   39

National Data Collection on Police Use of Force

Data collection challenges   42

    Definitions of use of force   43
    Incident-level versus aggregate-level data
      submission   49
    Rates of police use of force   52
    Misapplications of use of force data   55
    Anonymity of submitting agencies   59

Alternative approaches to data collection   60
    Official records   63
      Court records   63
      Citizen complaint records   64
      Arrest records   66
      Use-of-force reports   68
      Injury records   69
    Surveys of police   71
    Surveys of citizens   73

National data collection efforts   75
    Victimization study   75
    IACP study   78

Conclusions   82

References   83

Public databases   89

Appendix   91

Foreword

This report highlights findings from existing research on police use of force. It describes how the Bureau of Justice Statistics and the National Institute of Justice will collect data on police contacts with members of the public that result in the use of force by law enforcement officers. The report responds to Section 210402 of the Violent Crime Control and Law Enforcement Act of 1994, which requires the Attorney General to "acquire data about the use of excessive force by law enforcement officers" and to "publish an annual summary of the data acquired. . . ."

Systematically collecting information on use of force from the Nation's more than 17,000 law enforcement agencies is difficult given the lack of standard definitions, the variety of incident recording practices, and the sensitivity of the issue. However, BJS and NIJ have embarked on several projects to improve our knowledge of police use of force:

• BJS is field testing a national household survey to assess how often police-public contacts result in use of force. The survey will ask approximately 100,000 people each year to describe any recent contact they may have had with the police and will be the first comprehensive collection of information about all kinds of experiences in contacting the police, positive as well as negative. Some fraction of these contacts

National Data Collection on Police Use of Force

will involve police use of force, permitting further analysis to ascertain the incidence and characteristics of police use of excessive force.

• BJS and NIJ are sponsoring the National Police Use of Force Database, currently administered by the International Association of Chiefs of Police. This pilot project will use a standard form to gather information directly from law enforcement agencies on incidents involving use of force.

• NIJ is funding several site-specific research projects on use of force. One project will survey arresting officers in four cities about the kind of force used and the circumstances of arrest.

The Bureau of Justice Statistics, the National Institute of Justice, and the Institute for Law and Justice cooperated to bring you this report. We hope you will find it valuable in understanding what is known about police use of force, and the measures that can be taken to improve that understanding.

Jan M. Chaiken
Director
Bureau of Justice Statistics

Jeremy Travis
Director
National Institute of Justice

National Data Collection on Police Use of Force

Introduction

The feature distinguishing police from all other groups in society is their authority to apply coercive force when circumstances call for it. Police may be called on to use force when making an arrest, breaking up an altercation, dispersing an unruly crowd, or performing a myriad of other official activities during their daily routines. The force may range from pushing a person to get his attention to using a firearm. Between those extremes are several other types of force, including firm grips on an arm, use of debilitating chemical agents, and blows with a baton. Whatever method is used, police are expected to apply only the force necessary to resolve a given situation.

When police go beyond reasonable force to use *excessive* force during an arrest or in precipitous response, as during the decades of protest demonstrations involving labor, civil rights, or other controversial issues, citizens become victims of police, and the public's confidence in a police force can plummet. Known abuses of force rightfully receive extensive attention from the public, politicians, media, and, in some cases, civil and even criminal courts. While condemning the incidents of excessive force, law enforcement officials note that not enough attention and credit is given to the police when they successfully resolve situations without any use of force or with only minimal force.

The basic problem is the lack of routine, national systems for collecting data on incidents in which police use force during the normal course of duty and on the extent of excessive force. Some observers believe that abuses of force reaching the attention of the public and the media are only the tip of the iceberg. They point, for example, to recent revelations in several large cities that some officers routinely beat up drug suspects and falsify evidence. Other observers note that police resolve literally millions of incidents each year without resorting to force and believe that the incidence of excessive force has been blown out of proportion. William A. Geller, a well-known researcher on police use of force, summarizes the views of these observers in saying, "If known abuses are the tip of an iceberg, then commendable restraint when officers could have applied force is like the zenith of Mt. Everest." Regardless of viewpoint, everyone agrees that excessive force has an adverse impact on relationships between police and the communities they serve, and seemingly no one would agree that ignorance on this topic is bliss.

The lack of reliable data on the extent of excessive force received the attention of the United States Congress in enacting the Violent Crime Control and Law Enforcement Act of 1994. The Act requires the Attorney General to collect data on excessive force by police and to publish an annual report from the data (Title XXI, Subtitle D, Police Pattern or Practice):

> Section 210402. Data on Use of Excessive Force.
> (a) The Attorney General shall, through appropriate means, acquire data about the use of excessive force by law enforcement officers.
> (b) Data acquired under this section shall be used only for research or statistical purposes and may not contain any information that may reveal the identity of the victim or any law enforcement officer.
> (c) The Attorney General shall publish an annual summary of the data acquired under this section.

This discussion paper represents the first response to provide information annually on police use of force. It summarizes what is known from prior research studies that have looked at police use of force and gathered data on the incidence of police force. Difficulties encountered by researchers and police executives in collecting use-of-force data are described in this report, including variations in definitions of police use of force, reluctance by police agencies to provide reliable data, concerns about the misapplication of reported data, and the degree of detail needed on individual incidents.

Federally funded efforts by the Bureau of Justice Statistics (BJS) and the National Institute of Justice (NIJ) are now underway to collect national data on police use of force in a routine manner. This report describes these efforts along with their approaches to overcome the difficulties of past data collection efforts. Subsequent annual reports will provide results from these federally funded activities.

Police Use of Force Workshop

In May 1995, the National Institute of Justice and the Bureau of Justice Statistics convened a Police Use of Force Workshop to discuss the provisions of Section 210402. The workshop brought together over 40 experts, including chiefs of police, lawyers, researchers, police union representatives, federal agency representatives, police trainers, and civilian review board representatives. (See Appendix, page 92, for the list of participants.) They discussed the obstacles to acquiring data on excessive force and debated the most appropriate collection procedures.

Workshop participants noted that while the provisions of Section 210402 are well intentioned, acquiring data on the use of excessive force is difficult. First, there is no single, accepted definition of "excessive force" among police, researchers, and legal analysts.[1] The legal test for excessive force is whether the officer *reasonably* believed such force to be *necessary* to

---

[1] See, for example, Geoffrey P. Alpert and William C. Smith, "How Reasonable Is the Reasonable Man? Police and Excessive Force," *The Journal of Criminal Law and Criminology,* 85(2) Fall 1994: 481-501. The problem even extends to the definition of use of deadly force; see William A. Geller and Michael S. Scott, *Deadly Force: What We Know: A Practitioner's Desk Reference on Police-Involved Shootings* (Washington: Police Executive Research Forum, 1992).

accomplish a legitimate police purpose.[2] Becausethere
are no universally accepted definitions of what is "reasonable" and "necessary," it becomes necessary for ju-
rors and jurists to make decisions on the presentations
in each individual case. The case-by-case
approach is not unusual in our jurisprudence system
where legal definitions are unclear and the surrounding circumstances may be open to differing opinions.[3]

Even if a definition were agreed on, questions would
still exist about the best source for determining the
incidence of excessive force. Three obvious sources
of data would be the public, the police, and the courts,
but each presents difficulties. How can we survey the
public to obtain the information? Will police cor-
rectly apply a common definition to all reported incidents of force and report all such incidents? Are cases
that reach the courts really the best gauge for the incidence of excessive force? Will it be possible to establish a national database on police use of force? How

---

[2] See Neal Miller, "Less-Than-Lethal Force Weaponry: Law
Enforcement and Correctional Agency Civil Law Liability for
the Use of Excessive Force," *Creighton Law Review,* Vol. 28,
No. 3, April 1995, pp. 733-94; and Antony M. Pate and Lorie
A. Fridell, *Police Use of Force: Official Reports, Citizen
Complaints and Legal Consequences* (Washington: Police
Foundation, 1993); and *Graham* v. *Connor,* 490 U.S. 386
(1989).

[3] This case-by-case approach can be distinguished from criminal
cases, such as burglaries, in which proof of illegal entry into a
premises may be most easily established as factual evidence that
a law has been broken.

can we obtain the support of law enforcement agencies in collecting data on force applied by its officers?

Overarching these issues is the appropriateness of collecting data only on "excessive force" by police. Most attendees at the workshop indicated the need for data on all police use of force. Police representatives stated that the aim of progressive police agencies is to minimize *use of force* by its officers, not just to reduce *excessive force*. Indeed, data collection on all uses of force would assist in measuring changes over time and in improving programs for training recruits and current officers. Police executives could have better relationships with their public constituents by making full disclosures on the incidence of force by officers and the circumstances under which force was needed.

Researchers also prefer collecting data on all uses of force rather than limiting the collection effort to incidents with excessive force. Indeed, virtually every major research study in this area has looked at the total picture rather than concentrating on excessive force. As pointed out by more than one workshop attendee, data on all uses of force can allow the analysis to proceed from scenarios in which minor force was applied to scenarios of excessive force. The gradations along the way provide researchers with a better picture of the circumstances under which police apply different types of force and what causes the escalation of incidents to excessive force. The result is better insight into how to minimize use of force and avoid circumstances leading to excessive use.

It was noted during the workshop that the provisions of Section 210402 do not limit the data collection to excessive force incidents. The provisions can therefore be viewed as a starting point for data collection, not as restricting the type of data that can be collected.

In summary, the Police Use of Force Workshop brought out several important points that subsequently assisted in molding decisions to satisfy the federal requirements. The first is that no single data collection mechanism can provide a full picture of police use of force. Several methodologies (use of court records, citizen complaints to police, use-of-force reports by officers, surveys of citizens, etc.) were discussed at the workshop. Each was viewed as having advantages and disadvantages.

A related point is that the lack of accepted definitions of *use of force* and *excessive force* will remain a fact of life even after a fuller understanding of these incidents is developed. As a consequence, it is important that any data collection effort provide enough detail to examine these issues under different definitions.

Finally, the aim of progressive police departments is to reduce the amount of force needed to resolve conflicts, not just to identify and deal with excessive force. Workshop participants therefore believed that the data collection should be expanded beyond the section's requirements.

Federal responses

National data collection efforts

As a result of the workshop, internal staff work at the Department of Justice, and a review of related research, NIJ and BJS have taken steps to directly address the requirements of Section 210402. They have jointly funded the development of a national database on police use of force based on information voluntarily provided by police departments. Under the grant project, the International Association of Chiefs of Police (IACP) will establish a National Use of Force Database Center to collect data from contributing police departments on their uses of force. Details on this effort are provided later in this paper.

BJS also intends to field test a police-public contact survey by expanding its National Crime Victimization Survey (NCVS) to include a series of questions about the use of both appropriate and inappropriate force during police-civilian encounters. The NCVS annually contacts a representative sample of more than 100,000 persons in the nation to obtain information from them about crime and its consequences. By adding questions about police use of force, the survey will obtain information from those who are directly affected by that force.

Annual summaries

As previously indicated, Section 210402 requires that the Attorney General publish an annual summary of data acquired on police use of force. This first report is in response to the annual requirement, but because the mechanisms for systematically acquiring data are not yet in place, the discussion is on what is known from prior research projects and the lessons learned from these studies on collecting and analyzing these data. Some of these research reports provide estimates in line with the aims of Section 210402 and all contribute to our understanding of the situations and circumstances under which police apply force. Summarizing the results from these reports therefore provides a framework for subsequent annual reports.

Most of what is known about the incidence of police use of force in this country is a result of projects funded by NIJ and BJS over the last 20 years. For example, NIJ funded several studies in the late 1970s and early 1980s on deadly force or "justifiable homicide" by police departments and the impact these serious incidents had on communities.[4] More recently,

---

[4]See, for example, Kenneth J. Metulia, *A Balance of Forces* (Washington: National Institute of Justice). This study by the International Association of Chiefs of Police, although criticized later for inconsistent data provided by some of the contributing police departments, provided an analysis of the trends over time in deadly force incidents and included several recommended guidelines for police departments.

NIJ sponsored a survey by Antony Pate and Lorie Fridell of a nationally representative sample of police departments to obtain statistics for 1991 on their incidence of uses of force and citizen complaints about force. This study was a comprehensive attempt to collect national statistics on the incidence of police use of force. Another recent publication, *And Justice For All: Understanding and Controlling Police Abuse of Force*, edited by William A. Geller and Hans Toch,[5] adds significantly to our understanding of the complexities surrounding police use of force through a series of contributed papers. Finally, an important perspective is provided by Joel Garner and John Buchanan,[6] whose NIJ-sponsored study examined use of force by and against police in Phoenix, Arizona. Its findings are presented later in this paper as an example of data collection at the local level.[7]

In 1993 and 1994, the Virginia Association of Chiefs of Police (VACOP) asked law enforcement agencies

---

[5]William A. Geller and Hans Toch, eds., *And Justice for All: Understanding and Controlling Police Abuse of Force* (Washington: Police Executive Research Forum, 1995).
[6]Joel Garner and John Buchanan, *Executive Summary: Understanding the Use of Force By and Against the Police* (Washington: National Institute of Justice, 1995).
[7]The Police Use of Force Workshop was also beneficial in preparation of this report because of the open discussion by participants on a variety of issues. However, workshop participants did not have an opportunity to review the report and individual participants may not necessarily endorse particular views stated in the report.

in the State to voluntarily provide data on their incidence of use of force.[8] While the response rates were relatively low, the organization's ability to initiate the study and obtain cooperation from responding departments is noteworthy. This study also laid the foundation for a grant award to the IACP for establishment of a national database on use-of-force data voluntarily provided by contributing police departments. The results of the VACOP study and a description of the IACP's forthcoming efforts are provided later in this report.

Research on police use of force

Two recent awards by NIJ will continue research on this important topic. One award will collect detailed data in four cities on the dynamics of incidents involving use of force from the viewpoint of both police officers and citizens. This project is a replication of the recently completed effort in Phoenix.

A second award funds Dr. Geoff Alpert at the University of South Carolina for an analysis of existing databases available from the Metro-Dade (Florida) Police Department and the cities of Eugene and Springfield, Oregon. During the years 1992-1994, the Metro-Dade Police Department completed 1,311 use-of-force reports. Each report contains information on the type

---

[8]Virginia Association of Chiefs of Police, *1994 Use of Force Report,* November 1994.

of force used, amount of citizen resistance, and extent of injuries or complaints of injuries. The databases from the Oregon cities are of interest because they were developed during a special study on the physical abilities that police officers require in order to perform essential and critical duties satisfactorily. For a one-month period, police officers completed "Police Officers' Physical Abilities Studies Job Task Analysis Data Collection" forms that included use of force by officers during incidents. The study will determine the relationship between the amount of resistance met by police and the amount of force used to control resisting subjects.

The remainder of this paper is organized in the following manner. The next section gives an overview on the general topics of police use of force, including summaries of early studies on police use of force, the need for local data collection on force, and the surprisingly high number of groups with interest in obtaining statistics on police use of force. Results from three recent studies on the incidence of police use of force are then presented as examples of national, State, and local statistical efforts. The difficulties in collecting data on police use of force are examined in a section that discusses various definitions of police use of force, concerns on how the data will be used, and other issues. Because several potential sources exist from which data could be collected, a section on the advantages and disadvantages of different data collection approaches has been included. The paper concludes with details on the two major initiatives by BJS and NIJ to collect national data on police use of force.

Police use of force: An overview

Prior studies of use of force

In his seminal study on the functions of police, Egon
Bittner established the need for police to use force
(from verbal force to deadly force) when required and
the expectation on the part of citizens that force will
be applied. In his words —

> [W]hatever the substance of the task at
> hand, whether it involves protection against
> an undesired imposition, caring for those
> who cannot care for themselves, attempting
> to solve a crime, helping to save a life,
> abating a nuisance, or settling an explosive
> dispute, police intervention means above all
> making use of the capacity and authority
> to overpower resistance to an attempted
> solution in the native habitat of the problem.
> There can be no doubt that this feature
> of police work is uppermost in the minds
> of people who solicit police aid or direct the
> attention of the police to problems, that
> persons against whom the police proceed
> have this feature in mind and conduct them-
> selves accordingly, and that every conceiv-
> able police intervention projects the message
> that force may be, and may have to be, used
> to achieve a desired objective. It does not
> matter whether the persons who seek police

help are private citizens or other government officials, nor does it matter whether the problem at hand involves some aspect of law enforcement or is totally unconnected with it.[9]

Early studies on the incidence of use of force focused on lethal, or deadly, force by police.[10] Lethal force, obviously the highest level of force used by police, results in the most severe injuries to its recipients and commands the greatest attention from the media. The early studies looked at the incidence and circumstances of lethal force in individual cities.

In 1977, the Police Foundation conducted a seven-city study of shooting incidents by police.[11] The cities included Birmingham, Alabama; Detroit, Michigan; Indianapolis, Indiana; Kansas City, Missouri; Oakland, California; Portland, Oregon; and Washington, D.C. The research team examined department policies on shootings, analyzed available reports, conducted extensive interviews, and rode in patrol cars as observers. Among their major findings was the observation that most departments were only

---

[9]Egon Bittner, *The Functions of Police in Modern Society* (Washington: National Institute of Mental Health, 1970), p. 40.
[10]See Geller and Scott for a comprehensive review of the last three decades' leading studies of deadly force used by and against police officers.
[11]Catherine H. Milton, Jeanne Wahl Halleck, James Lardner, and Gary L. Abrecht, *Police Use of Deadly Force* (Washington: Police Foundation, 1977).

beginning to develop recordkeeping procedures on police use of excessive force and repeated involvement of officers in shooting incidents. They went on to note, "The lack of systematic, centralized data collection in many departments inhibits the rational development of new policies, training programs, and enforcement procedures."[12]

The Police Foundation team called for a national effort to collect data on shooting incidents: "A reliable, national-level source of information about police-civilian shooting incidents is necessary so that states, cities, and police departments can review and objectively evaluate their laws, policies, and procedures affecting police use of deadly force."[13]

Simultaneously with its own seven-city inquiry, the Police Foundation helped underwrite the Chicago Law Enforcement Study Group's analysis of the Chicago (Illinois) Police Department's internal investigative files on officer-involved shootings, the first study in which a major city police department voluntarily opened its confidential files on shootings to a citizens' group. In offering a variety of recommendations for further inquiry on the nature and extent of proper and improper use of deadly force by Chicago officers, the study cautioned, "These inquiries will be possible only

---

[12]Milton, Halleck, Lardner, and Abrecht, p. 141.
[13]Ibid.

if the Police Department routinely collects and analyzes or permits others to collect and analyze the necessary data on police-involved shootings."[14]

In 1971, Albert Reiss reported observations he made while riding with police officers in Boston, Chicago, and Washington, D.C. His aim was to systematically record the circumstances of encounters between citizens and police. He noted, "Precise estimates of the extent to which the police engage in unwarranted conduct toward citizens are lacking."[15] While he did not attempt to determine the incidence of use of force by officers, his observations led him to conclude that police use of force is rare. He also commented on the overall circumstances that lead to police use of force: "There is evidence that many situations that provoke police to use undue force closely resemble those that give rise to assaults by private citizens. In both cases, the force is exerted in quick anger against real or imagined aggression."[16]

State task forces looking into use of force by local police departments have also called for improved data collection efforts. For example, a report in 1985 to then-Governor Mario Cuomo examined the use of deadly force by police in New York State. Among

[14]William A. Geller and Kevin J. Karales, *Split-Second Decisions: Shootings of and by Chicago Police* (Chicago: Chicago Law Enforcement Study Group, 1981), p. 201.
[15]Albert J. Reiss, Jr., *The Police and The Public* (New Haven, Connecticut: Yale University Press, 1971), p. 141.
[16]Ibid, p. 150.

its recommendations was this: "A centralized comprehensive reporting system on the discharge of firearms by police should be instituted through legislation. This would require police agencies to report the relevant information to the Division of Criminal Justice Services on a monthly basis."[17] In 1992, a task force on police use of force established by New Jersey's attorney general made this recommendation: "All law enforcement officers should be required to report, and all law enforcement agencies should be required to collect information about incidents involving use of force."[18] It went on to recommend that all law enforcement agencies prepare an annual use-of-force incident report and submit it to the county prosecutor. The summary report "should contain the total number of incidents involving the use of any force, the total number of incidents involving use of excessive force and the total number of firearms discharges."[19]

Several other researchers (Alpert and Fridell, 1992; Geller and Scott, 1992; Fyfe, 1988; Geller, 1985; Geller and Toch, 1995; Matulia, 1982; Sherman and Langworthy, 1979) have called for expanded databases at both the local and national level on all use

---

[17]Richard J. Condon, *Police Use of Deadly Force in New York State* (Albany, New York: Division of Criminal Justice Services, 1985), p. iv.
[18]Frederick P. DeVesa, *Report of the Attorney General's Task Force on the Use of Force in Law Enforcement* (Trenton, New Jersey: 1992), p. 47.
[19]*Ibid.*

of force, not just lethal force. Their calls for national databases went unheeded until the 1994 Crime Act.

It should be noted, however, that a national database of a more restrictive and less consistent nature already exists. The FBI collects voluntarily submitted data on deaths from police actions for its Supplementary Homicide Reports. It disseminates the data only on request, and summaries of those deaths are not part of the FBI's annual Uniform Crime Reports. Several studies have noted problems with this limited data collection effort, most notably the inconsistencies between numbers reported to the FBI and numbers reported in other data collection efforts.[20]

One way of organizing data collection and analysis falls under the category of a *force continuum*, which envisions a range of options available to police officers from verbalization techniques to deadly force. In the middle of that range lies the variety of less-than-lethal weapons now available to police. Tom McEwen and Frank Leahy[21] discuss several types

---

[20]See James J. Fyfe, "Police Use of Deadly Force: Research and Reform," *Justice Quarterly,* 5(2) 1988: 165-201; Lawrence W. Sherman and Robert H. Langworthy, "Measuring Homicide by Police Officers," *The Journal of Criminal Law and Criminology,* 70(4) 1979: 546-560; and Geller and Scott.
[21]Tom McEwen and Frank Leahy, *Final Report: Less Than Lethal Force Technologies in Law Enforcement and Correctional Agencies* (Washington: National Institute of Justice, 1994).

of less-than-lethal weapons under four general categories:

- Impact weapons (for instance, batons and flashlights)
- Chemical weapons (for example, pepper spray)
- Electrical weapons (for instance, electronic stun guns)
- Other less-than-lethal weapons (such as stunning devices and projectile launchers)

In their survey of police departments and sheriffs' agencies, McEwen and Leahy found that 93% reported at least one type of impact weapon available, 71% had chemical weapons, and 16% had electrical weapons.[22]

With regard to the incidence of use of less-than-lethal technologies, an article in the *Law Enforcement News* reported that use of pepper spray — a cayenne pepper-based chemical spray — by New York City police officers has increased dramatically with use of the spray in 603 arrests during the first 10 months of 1995, compared to 217 uses for the same period in 1994.[23] By comparison, nightsticks were employed 188 times

---

[22]McEwen and Leahy, pp. 6-7.
[23]"OC Spray is New York City Cops' Weapon of Choice," *Law Enforcement News*, XXII(438), January 31, 1996, p. 5.

during the same 10 months of 1995, and 158 times in 1994.

The proliferation of these less-than-lethal technologies, especially chemical agents such as pepper spray, expands the data collection effort on use of force. Any data collection system needs to include the variety of weapons available to the police.

Data reporting needs and police liability

The need for improved data collection systems can also be justified by considering the legal liabilities that law enforcement agencies have with their use of force, from both lethal and less-than-lethal weapons. Writing in the *Creighton Law Review*, Neal Miller states that the general principles of tort law applicable to peace officers' use of any force apply equally to lethal and less-than-lethal weapons. The general principle is that the appropriateness of law enforcement uses of force is measured legally by the objective reasonableness of the officers' actions. This general principle combines with other factors unique to law enforcement, for example —

• Peace officers are responsible for responding to the medical needs of subjects against whom force was used.

• Supervisors and line officers have a duty to intervene when another officer is using excessive force against a subject.

Governmental liability for civil torts of its law enforcement personnel also has unique features, not applicable to private employers:

• The doctrine of *respondeat superior*, whereby the employer is responsible for the acts of its employees, is not applicable to governmental bodies. Instead, State "tort claim acts" regulate and limit municipal libability for employee torts. Acts covered by these laws include simple negligence, endangerment of third parties, and even minor assaults.

• Governmental liability under Federal law exists only where there is a causal relationship between a governmental failure, such as inadequate training or supervision of police officers who are the subject of multiple excessive force allegations. Typically, Federal excessive force cases involve either serious assault charges or a series of excessive force incidents.

• Governmental bodies in most states are responsible for indemnifying peace officers against whom court damages have been levied, except in the most egregious cases of excessive force. [24]

Miller concludes his extensive discussion on liability issues with recommendations on reporting needs for law enforcement agencies. While his discussion is limited to less-than-lethal weapons, the recommendations on reporting apply equally to use of lethal force. From a liability viewpoint, he recommends that officers prepare reports on all use-of-force incidents. These reports should include a description of what led up to the incident, what force was used, effectiveness of the force used, injuries sustained (if any), and medical assistance rendered. The report should allow inferences about how the use of less-than-lethal force prevented injuries to officers and obviated deadly

---

[24]Miller, p. 738.

force. If police departments maintain these reports, a logical next step is to use them to improve training, policies, and procedures on the appropriate uses of force.

In summary, the research conducted over the last 30 years on police use of force consistently calls for improved data collection at the local and national level. Increases in the availability and use of less-than-lethal weapons add to the need for data collection.

Consumers of police use of force data[25]

Assuming that local and national databases on use of force exist, it is logical to ask who would be interested in the available statistics and what the most appropriate uses of those statistics would be.

Groups with interest in statistics on police use of force

U.S. Department of Justice
Governors, legislators, and State attorneys general
Mayors, city managers, city council members, and prosecutors
Police chiefs and other law enforcement executives
Police rank-and-file organizations
Police support groups
Police oversight groups
Civilian review boards
Civil and human rights organizations
Newspapers, television, and other news media
General public
Good-government groups
Researchers in criminology, sociology, psychology, public administration, political science, and other fields

---

Exhibit 1

As reflected in Exhibit 1, data on use of force are of interest to a gamut of public and private stakeholders. Public officials want data on police use of force as it relates to their responsibilities. Police executives want

---

[25]The discussion in this section is a summary of Mr. William Geller's remarks at the Police Use of Force Workshop.

data on use of force because of their unique role in controlling its application. The police rank and file want information on their members' use of force to illustrate restraint, identify professionalism, and help protect officers' rights in after-action review procedures. Other local groups, such as oversight agencies, need statistics on use of force as part of their mandate to keep watch over police. Researchers in several related fields — criminology, sociology, psychology, public administration, and political science — want data on police use of force as a basis for analyzing the factors surrounding its application and determining how police can minimize it. Finally, the news media have a natural interest in police use of force because it is their job to report newsworthy items to the public.

The particular interests of these groups differ. Police executives have a special need to improve the training of recruits and police officers on the use of force and techniques to minimize its application. They also want to improve officer safety. There is a well-founded belief among police executives and researchers that officers generally exercise restraint in their use of force and that incidents of excessive force represent only a small portion of police-citizen encounters (see, for example, Reiss [1971], Friedrich [1980], and Worden [1995]). A data collection system on use of force could support that claim, which, without reliable data, is only conjecture. Such statistics would improve public attitudes toward police where those attitudes are negative as a result of isolated but widely publicized incidents. A police department may even find it easier to defend itself against lawsuits with information on use of force. The data might also guide decisions on the placement of officers with tendencies to use force to resolve confrontations. The data would also assist in decisions on policies and procedures for weapons such as batons, pepper spray, and other less-than-lethal weapons.

On the other hand, civilian oversight boards have a different interest in data on police use of force. They represent the viewpoints of the public, members of which might be the subject of coercive force by the police.

An important feature of reliable databases on use of force is that they would allow for a review of the *proper* use of force. Scant information is available on incidents in which the use of less-than-lethal force made it possible for police to avoid applying lethal force. Anecdotal information suggests that police officers typically make reasonable and careful decisions on their selection of force in most situations.

The aforementioned groups are likely frustrated by their inability to obtain complete and reliable information on incidents of police use of force. Even the number of major incidents of use of excessive force is unknown, and our knowledge of the overall incidence of use of force is gained only by occasional, expensive studies that provide "snapshots" of incidents and patterns during fixed periods. Until more reliable databases are established, the controversies over the improper use of force will continue.

Recent studies on police use of force

Three recently completed studies illustrate the variety of approaches to collecting data on police use of force and show the importance of definitions. The studies are Police Use of Force by Antony Pate and Lorie Fridell, 1994 Use of Force Report by the Virginia Association of Chiefs of Police, and Understanding the Use of Force By and Against the Police by Joel Garner and John Buchanan. They are, in turn, Federal, State, and local studies on police use of force. The Federal and local studies were supported through grants awarded by NIJ, while the State study fell under the auspices of the IACP's State Associations of Chiefs of Police (SACOP) organization. The studies show that there are several ways to collect data on use of force from police departments, each with advantages and disadvantages. They also provide insight into the problems that are likely to be encountered in future studies and suggest ways those problems can be overcome.

Unfortunately, the studies' results are not comparable. The data were collected during different periods, and the results in the final reports are presented in different ways. The Pate and Fridell study received 1,111 completed surveys from law enforcement agencies providing data for 1991 on use of force and citizen complaints. Most of the results in the final report are calculations on the number of incidents involving force per 1,000 sworn personnel. The VACOP study is based on a sample of police departments in Virginia during 1993 and again in 1994 on use of force, and the Garner and Buchanan study is based on a survey of 1,585 adult custody arrests completed by the Phoenix Police Department during two weeks in June 1994.

National survey of police use of force

To obtain a national picture on police use of force, Pate and Fridell selected a representative sample of 1,697 law enforcement agencies (1,016 municipal police departments, 588 county sheriffs' departments, 50 state police agencies, and 43 county police departments) from the total universe of 15,801 agencies in the United States. The agencies also represented four population categories (below 10,000; 10,000 to 24,999; 25,000 to 49,999; and 50,000 and over). The surveys, mailed to the 1,697 agencies in August 1992, asked for police use-of-force data for the previous year. After a series of follow-up activities, the researchers received 1,111 completed surveys (a 65.5 percent response rate), which were placed into a computer-readable format for analysis.

The survey asked about a wide range of degrees of force, from firm grips to firearms. The number of sworn officers was also requested so that rates of the use of force per 1,000 officers could be calculated. The results from the surveys were statistically weighted based on the number of agencies in the population by type of agency and population category.

Exhibit 2 shows the weighted survey results for reported incidents of police use of force per 1,000
sworn officers in city police departments (the largest
category of agencies).[26] The order of the results is
generally in line with the degree of force. That is, less
serious types of force, such as handcuffs and bodily
force, occur more frequently than more serious types
of force, such as vehicle rammings and shooting of
citizens.

The Pate and Fridell study also asked respondents to
provide the number of citizen complaints of excessive
force received by the agencies and the number of
those complaints that were sustained.[27] Citizen complaints to law enforcement are one source for measuring perceived excessive use of force, although no
claim is made that they provide the complete answer.

Exhibit 3 shows the rate of citizen complaints about
force for the responding city police departments
by sex of the complainants.[28] A summary calculation
gives a rate of 11.3 complaints per 100,000 population. An interesting feature of Exhibit 3 is that
although males represent only 48 percent of the

---

[26]Pate and Fridell, Table 6.1, p. 74. Pate and Fridell caution in
their report that not all departments responding to this survey
required their officers to report all uses of force.
[27]For their survey, excessive force was defined as "police use of
more force than is necessary in seizing or detaining an
individual."
[28]Pate and Fridell, Table 8.3, p. 95.

Reported incidents of police use of force per 1,000 sworn officers during 1991 in city departments

Type of force	Rate per 1,000 sworn officers
Handcuff/leg restraint	490.4
Bodily force (arm, foot, or leg)	272.2
Come-alongs	226.8
Unholstering weapon	129.9
Swarm	126.7
Twist locks/wrist locks	80.9
Firm grip	57.7
Chemical agents (Mace or Cap-Stun)	36.2
Batons	36.0
Flashlights	21.7
Dog attacks or bites	6.5
Electrical devices (TASER)	5.4
Civilians shot at but not hit	3.0
Other impact devices	2.4
Neck restraints/unconsciousness-rendering holds	1.4
Vehicle rammings	1.0
Civilians shot and killed	0.9
Civilians shot and wounded but not killed	0.2

Exhibit 2

general population, they account for 73 percent of the complaints and 83 percent of the sustained complaints. Males are therefore overrepresented in making complaints and sustained complaints compared to their numbers in the general population, but this result very likely reflects the overrepresentation of males in encounters with police concerning suspected crimes.

In summary, the Pate and Fridell study represents a one-year snapshot of police use of force. The research team made extensive calculations on police use of force as reported by the responding agencies and on excessive use of force as reflected by complaints to the agencies.

Complaints and sustained complaints of excessive force for city police departments during 1991

	Number	Percent	Number of responding agencies
General population	27,036,089		215
Male	12,910,899	48	
Female	14,125,190	52	
Complaints	3,053		215
Male	2,224	73	
Female	829	27	
Sustained complaints	480		73
Male	398	83	
Female	82	17	

Exhibit 3

National Data Collection on Police Use of Force 35

State survey of police use of force

In 1993 and 1994, the Virginia Association of Chiefs of Police (VACOP) sent Use of Force Survey forms to 360 law enforcement agencies in Virginia. The forms asked for data from the previous year. VACOP received 58 completed surveys of 1992 incidents and 83 surveys of 1993 incidents, for response rates of 16.1 percent and 23.1 percent, respectively. While those response rates are much lower than VACOP desired and undermined the anticipated representativeness of the findings, the increase in response is encouraging.

Results from the most recent survey include the following:

• The responding agencies made a total of 1,101,877 arrests and used force in 1,697 arrests, or about 0.15 percent of the total. The survey from the previous year showed that 0.3 percent of arrests involved force.

• A total of 897 officers were assaulted during the year, 26 of whom were off duty at the time.

• Seventy-eight of the 83 responding agencies required written reports on all instances of use of force.

• The agencies received a total of 119 complaints
from citizens about use of force, of which 99 complaints were determined to be unfounded and 20 were
sustained. An additional 25 complaints were made
from within the agencies, of which 19 complaints
were determined to be unfounded and 6 were
sustained.

• The median age of officers receiving complaints was
31 years, and the median length of experience was 7
years.

The interesting feature of the VACOP study lies in the
organization's willingness and ability to initiate the
study and its learning about the difficulties that even
police professional associations encounter in trying
to obtain cooperation from member agencies. On the
other hand, the study had two significant limitations.
The more obvious is the low response rate to the survey. The results may not be representative of all
agencies in the State. In addition, the definition of
police force is unclear in the study's report.

VACOP representatives at the Police Use of Force
Workshop indicated that their initial motivation was a
belief that police across the country do an outstanding
job of resolving literally millions of encounters without resorting to any force. However, no data existed
to prove or disprove their point. One VACOP representative stated during the meeting, "I don't believe
police use of force is a widespread problem, but until

we get the data, we can't prove it." Study results, however preliminary, have also proven useful with the Virginia General Assembly. Those results have restored a degree of police accountability, and the General Assembly now seeks advice from VACOP representatives on other matters.

Other participants at the meeting supported the view about the extent of police use of force. One motivation for agencies to contribute data to a national database may be to show that use of excessive force, while still serious whenever it occurs, is not a frequent event.

Local survey of police use of force

During two weeks in June 1994, a research team in Phoenix collected data on 1,585 adult custody arrests to measure the extent and types of force applied by and against police officers in the Phoenix Police Department.[29] These arrests represented 85% of the total adult custody arrests for the two-week period, and purposely did not include citation and warrant arrests. The study aimed at describing the amount of force used and the characteristics of arrest situations in which force was applied. Officers completed a two-page form on adults arrested and taken into custody during the 2-week period. The form included sections for recording types of force used (voice, restraints, and weapons), injuries given and received, and medical attention given and received.

As stated in the executive summary of the final report —

> During arrests in this study, officers used threats or shouts less than 4% of the time, pursued a fleeing suspect 7% of the time, placed handcuffs or restraints on 77% of the suspects, used a weaponless tactic (holding, hitting, etc.) 17% of the time, threatened

[29]The research team included Joel Garner and Jeffrey Fagan (Rutgers University); Tom Schade, John Hepburn, and Aogan Mulcahy (Arizona State University); and John Buchanan and Richard Groeneveld (Phoenix Police Department).

to use a weapon in 3.7% of the arrests, and used a weapon in 2 percent of the arrests. The most frequent weapon threatened was a handgun (45 arrests); the most frequent weapon used was a flashlight (12 arrests). In 20% of the adult custody arrests, no restraint was used.[30]

The research team also developed three measures of force used by police officers: physical force, a continuum of force, and maximum force. Similar measures were developed for force used by suspects. As an example of the results, 22% of the arrests involved physical force by police and 14% involved physical force by arrestees. For arrestees, physical force included —
(1) use of any weaponless tactic (grabbing, pushing, hitting, etc.) and
(2) use, threatened use, or possession of a weapon.
For police, physical force meant —
(1) use of severe restraints (handcuffs, hobbles, leg cuffs, and body restraints),
(2) use of any weaponless tactic, and
(3) use or threatened use of a weapon.

---

[30]Garner and Buchanan, p. 6.

The research team drew three important inferences from their study:

• Force is used infrequently by Phoenix police officers and, when used, is typically at the lower end of the defined measures of force.

• The single most frequent weapon used in arrests is the flashlight. This result raises concerns about training because the current training program provides limited guidance on the use of a flashlight as a weapon.

• The single best predictor of police use of force is whether the suspect used force. Other predictors of police use of force are these: the suspect is involved with a gang; the suspect is impaired by alcohol; the suspect is known to be resistive, assaultive, or armed with a weapon; both the suspect and police officer are male; and the offense suspected is violent.

Data collection challenges

Collection of data on police use of force presents several difficulties, starting with issues of definition. In this section, we explore five key data collection issues:

- Definitions of use of force
- Incident versus aggregate level data submission
- Rates of police use of force
- Misapplications of use-of-force data
- Anonymity of submitting agencies

The purpose of this section is to raise issues, not to provide solutions. Indeed, each of the topics has already received considerable discussion in the literature and will be the subject of research and debate for many more years. It is important, however, to understand the concerns of law enforcement administrators, researchers, and federal agencies regarding what data are needed and how those data will eventually be used. Decisions on those issues will eventually shape the collection of national statistics on police use of force.

Definitions of use of force

In deciding what data are to be collected and how, three terms must be differentiated: *police use of force, excessive use of force,* and *use of excessive force.* The differences are more than an exercise in twisting words and lie at the core of data collection issues.

Jerome H. Skolnick and James J. Fyfe note the following about the need for the use of force in police work:

> As long as some members of society do not comply with law and resist the police, force will remain an inevitable part of policing. Cops, especially, understand that. Indeed, anybody who fails to understand the centrality of force to police work has no business in a police uniform.[31]

While most police administrators and social scientists would agree with that statement, they would undoubtedly differ on exactly what constitutes force. Skolnick and Fyfe start with the *mere presence* of uniformed officers and marked patrol cars as expressions of force because they affect citizens' conduct. Force escalates from there to polite verbalization (for instance, persuasively asking someone to do something), strong verbal commands (direct orders in a commanding

---

[31]Jerome H. Skolnick and James J. Fyfe, *Above the Law: Police and the Excessive Use of Force* (New York: The Free Press, 1993), p. 37.

voice), firm grips on parts of the body (for example, moving someone along by gripping the elbow or shoulder), pain compliance techniques (hammer-locks or finger grips, for instance), impact techniques (for example, with kicks or batons), use of less-than-lethal weapons (chemical sprays or electronic stun guns, for example), and use of deadly weapons (discharge of firearms).

Any data collection effort on police use of force requires decisions on the specific types of force that will be included. In their study on force, Pate and Fridell collected data on the use of electrical devices (TASERs and stun guns), chemical agents (Mace and pepper spray), batons, metal flashlights, twist locks/ wrist locks,[32] swarms,[33] firm grips, neck restraints or unconsciousness-rendering holds (carotid sleeper or choke hold), handcuffs, leg restraints, come-alongs,[34] dog attacks,[35] vehicle rammings, and firearms. The list reflects the diversity of approaches available to police in applying force and the compre-hensiveness needed in a data collection effort on police use of force.[36]

---

[32]These are techniques involving twisting the wrist of a suspect.
[33]Several officers surround, immobilize, and handcuff a suspect.
[34]Application of a pain-inflicting hold to the hand or wrist to compel movement.
[35]Use of K-9 dogs to chase and disable a suspect.
[36]Pate and Fridell, p. 63.

For some people, the inclusion of flashlights and vehicle rammings may raise eyebrows because we do not ordinarily think of metal flashlights and vehicles as weapons. Departments issue flashlights for the specific purpose of providing illumination. However, the flashlight may be the only item available to an officer in an emergency. Research shows that metal flashlights have the potential to produce more bodily harm than most batons.[37] Most police department policies prohibit the use of metal flashlights except for illumination and as defensive weapons when absolutely necessary and only until other means become available. Metal flashlights, batons, and other blunt objects, when used for head strikes, are typically recognized as lethal weapons.

Police pursuits of suspects in vehicles, so-called *hot pursuits*, occur when suspects in vehicles leave the scene rather than face a police officer. A pursuit ensues if the officer feels obligated to stop the suspect, and some pursuits end when the police vehicle rams the other vehicle. Many police guidelines state that a pursuit should not begin, or should be terminated, when the risk created by driving exceeds the need for immediate apprehension of the suspect. In an insightful analysis of issues surrounding pursuits, Alpert and

---

[37]Terry C. Cox, Jerry S. Faughn, and William M. Nixon, "Police Use of Metal Flashlights as Weapons: An Analysis of Relevant Problems," *Journal of Police Science and Administration,* 13(3) 1985: 244-50.

Fridell (1992) view police vehicles and firearms as police instruments of deadly force.[38]

Use of excessive force means that police applied too much force in a given incident, while *excessive use of force* means that police apply force legally in too many incidents. Beyond the fact that force pertains to any of the above instruments, researchers do not agree on how to measure and obtain data on these two important topics. For example, Carl B. Klockars defines *excessive force* as "the use of any more force than a highly skilled police officer should find necessary to use in that particular situation."[39] To be sure, his prescription is not that departments punish officers, but that they help enhance officers' professionalism when high standards are not quite met. Fyfe distinguishes between two types of excessive force.

Extralegal violence (i.e., brutality) is "the willful and wrongful use of force by officers who knowingly exceed the bounds of their office," while *unnecessary force* "occurs when well-meaning officers prove incapable of dealing with the situations they encounter without needless or too hasty resort to force."[40]

---

[38]Geoffrey P. Alpert and Lorie A. Fridell, *Police Vehicles and Firearms: Instruments of Deadly Force* (Prospect Heights, Illinois: Waveland Press, Inc., 1992).

[39]Carl B. Klockars, "A Theory of Excessive Force and Its Control," in *And Justice for All,* pp. 17-18.

[40]James J. Fyfe, "Training to Reduce Police-Civilian Violence," in *And Justice for All*, p. 163.

Regardless of the specific definition, researchers face many problems on how to collect data about excessive force. The primary problem is that classifying an incident as involving excessive force is a judgment call. The "facts" of an incident are subject to interpretation, especially when police and citizens view circumstances differently. Police will sometimes disagree among themselves, although often not publicly, about what constitutes appropriate coercive force in a given situation. Therefore, classification errors will inevitably occur, and the impact of those errors will depend on the eventual use of the resulting data.

The incidence of *excessive use of force* should be important to police departments because it may serve as an indicator of weak policies on use of force; weak enforcement of policies; inadequate training, supervision, or equipment; or potentially violent police officers. As Geller and Toch point out, the officer "who uses legitimate force quite often may be a folk hero to many in the organization and the neighborhood but is generally understood by thoughtful, experienced practitioners to be tempting fate."[41] The 1991 report by the Independent Commission on the Los Angeles

---

[41]William A. Geller and Hans Toch, "Improving Our Understanding and Control of Police Abuse of Force: Recommendations for Research and Action," in *And Justice for All*, p. 279.

Police Department (usually called the Christopher Commission report), concluded that officers who use force at an above average rate may tend eventually to use excessive force. That is, excessive use of force may lead to use of excessive force.

Incident-level versus aggregate-level data submission

Assuming that acceptable definitions are developed, information on police use of force could be provided to a national database in two ways. One approach is to provide detailed data on each incident in which police force was applied or on each person against whom or by whom force was applied. Data could include date, time, number of officers involved, type of encounter, officer characteristics (age, race, sex, number of years in department), participant characteristics (age, race, sex), and other important descriptors.

The other way — the aggregate approach — is to provide tabulations on the number of incidents in which police force was applied or the number of persons against whom or by whom force was applied. The amount of data would be more limited than with incident-level data. Aggregate data might include, for example, only the tabulations by month, type of encounter, and individual participant or officer characteristics (age, race, sex).

Incident-level data provide a richer database for analysis and minimize the risk of overlooking important nuances of police-citizen encounters. Numerous cross-tabulations can be developed showing, for example, the relationships between characteristics of officers and participants by types of encounters. The disadvantage is that requesting incident-level data places a greater burden on local police departments, which must collect the details of each incident. However, progressive police agencies may already collect such data for purposes of internal efforts to upgrade performance.

Tabulating data at the aggregate level does not necessarily require having incident data because tallies can be made with work sheets. Small departments may find it easier to develop aggregate data because they have proportionately fewer incidents to report. The disadvantage is that aggregate data limit the variety and depth of analysis. Cross-tabulations are restricted to the tables provided in the data collection phase.

By way of comparison, law enforcement agencies can now provide UCR data as either incident records or aggregated data. The traditional approach is at the aggregate level and is accomplished by providing UCR data in the form of monthly tabulations on the number of crimes by category and on the number of arrests by crime category, sex, race, and age. Since January 1989, the FBI has accepted data in an incident format under the National Incident-Based Reporting System (NIBRS). NIBRS has been introduced because of a strongly held belief that eventual use of an incident-based system is needed to address a number of pressing national, State, and local policy questions about crime and its control. Law enforcement agencies choosing the NIBRS approach must provide the data in a format described in FBI publications.[42] Law enforcement acceptance of the NIBRS program has been limited, especially among large agencies.

---

[42]See *Volume 1: Data Collection Guidelines, National Incident-Based Reporting System,* Federal Bureau of Investigation, July 1988.

Rates of police use of force

After collecting use-of-force data, one of the most
common analytical tools for making sense of the
wealth of information obtained is the calculation of
rates. However, an understanding of the underlying
features of rates is important, especially when underlying incidents involve several officers and subjects.
For example, three officers arriving at a bar fight may
arrest four people and use force on two of them. The
incident may be viewed as a single encounter involving use of force, as two arrests with force and two
arrests without force, or as three officers using force.
The usual data collection guideline is to capture all information about the incident so that tabulations and
rates can be determined. Tabulations show one view
of the data by indicating the number of incidents with
use of force, the number of arrestees against whom
force was applied, and the number of officers who
used force. As with the Christopher Commission
report, the conclusion might be that a small number
of officers account for a majority of the uses of force.

Calculating rates requires more information but provides a better picture and reduces the risks of unfair
comparisons between jurisdictions. The numerator
for a rate may be the number of persons, number
of officers, number of arrests, or number of incidents
involving force for a given period. The denominator
represents the corresponding total number of persons,
officers, arrests, or incidents for the same period. The

rate for a given period, such as a month, is simply the quotient of these two numbers. While the number of arrests will change from one month to the next, the use-of-force rate may remain constant. The rates may be useful for several reasons, including the determination of excessive use of force, identification of officers with higher than average rates and detection of rate increases, which may indicate a need for training or policy changes.

The selection of the denominator may also depend on the objectives of a study or research project. For example, Pate and Fridell asked law enforcement agencies in their survey to provide the number of citizen complaints received during 1991 and the number of sworn officers in the department for that year. In their final report, they presented both the number of complaints received and the rate of complaints per 1,000 sworn officers. The rates provided a basis of comparison across departments of different sizes.

Other rates calculated by changing the denominator may also be useful to a police department. For example, rates could be calculated based on the number of calls for service, adult population in the jurisdiction, specific types of incidents (for instance, domestic situations), special populations (ages 18 to 24, for example), and others. The results might prove beneficial in allocating resources and in deciding how different types of situations should be handled.

It should be noted, however, that the use of rates to compare jurisdictions may be misleading when other factors are not taken into consideration. Two jurisdictions may differ considerably in demographic characteristics such as age distribution of the population, ethnic composition, economic base, and other factors. The rates may also differ simply because the police department in one jurisdiction has been more honest in its reporting on use of force. The same problems can occur even when comparisons are made between two different areas of the same city. The point is that the comparisons of rates can be beneficial but may need to take other factors into consideration.

Misapplications of use of force data

As indicated during the Police Use of Force Workshop, and reinforced by the experiences of the
VACOP project, police administrators and researchers
are concerned about the eventual misapplication of
data they provide on their use of force. The concerns
are predicated on the strong belief that comparisons
among cities are inevitable. As one participant ob-
served, "If you don't want comparisons, don't collect
the data."

Parallels with Uniform Crime Report statistics lend
credence to the concerns. The media regularly make
comparisons by using crime statistics. Articles on cities with the highest crime rates appear whenever the
FBI releases the annual UCR statistics. No police
chief wants to be labeled as heading the police department of the "number one crime capital" of the United
States. A chief might have even greater concern with
being labeled head of the department with the highest
rate of use of force against its citizens.

Comparisons can also be expected at the local level
because data on police use of force will likely be made
publicly available. Local media, civic groups, and
others will want to know if one area of the city has a
greater incidence of police use of force than others or
whether particular groups of citizens are dispropor-
tionately the subjects of force.

Another concern of law enforcement officers and researchers is the potential uses of these statistics by Federal agencies. By way of background, in October 1991, the House Committee on the Judiciary released a report on H.R. 3371 in which it addressed the Justice Department's lack of authority to address systemic patterns or practices of police misconduct. While the Department of Justice could prosecute individual officers for their actions, it could not bring action against a police department itself to correct an underlying problem, such as lack of training. As stated in the report,

> This [lack of authority to sue a local government or its officials] represents a serious and outdated gap in the federal scheme for protecting constitutional rights. The Attorney General has pattern or practice authority under eight civil rights statutes, including those governing voting, housing, employment, education, public accommodations and access to public facilities. The Justice Department can sue a city or county over its voter registration practices or its educational policies. It can sue private and public employers, including police departments, over patterns of employment discrimination. The Justice Department can seek injunctive relief under the Civil Rights of Institutionalized Persons Act against a jail or prison that tolerates guards beating inmates. But it cannot

sue to change the policy of a police department that tolerates officers beating citizens on the street.[43]

Section 210401 (Cause of Action) of the 1994 Crime Act addresses this omission with the following provisions:

(a) Unlawful Conduct. It shall be unlawful for any governmental authority, or any agent thereof, or any person acting on behalf of a governmental authority, to engage in a pattern or practice of conduct by law enforcement officers or by officials or employees of any governmental agency with responsibility for the administration of juvenile justice or the incarceration of juveniles that deprives persons of rights, privileges, or immunities secured or protected by the Constitution or laws of the United States.

(b) Civil Action by Attorney General. Whenever the Attorney General has reasonable cause to believe that a violation of paragraph (1) has occurred, the Attorney General, for or in the name of the United

---

[43]Committee on the Judiciary, U.S. House of Representatives, *Omnibus Crime Control Act of 1991: Report on H.R. 3371,* (1991), p. 137.

States, may in a civil action obtain appropriate equitable and declaratory relief to elimi-
nate the pattern or practice.

The concern expressed by some law enforcement representatives at the Police Use of Force Workshop is
that the data collected on excessive force under Section 210402 could be used by the Department of Justice to identify police departments that might be
engaging in a policy or practice falling under Section
210401. That is, if statistics on excessive force are
available at the Department of Justice on all police
departments, then an analysis of the data could readily
identify departments with high rates of excessive
force. A question was raised as to whether it was the
intent of Congress or of the Department of Justice that
such analysis of data collected under Section 210402
should result in civil action against specific departments under the provisions of Section 210401.

Anonymity of submitting agencies

One possible way to avoid the problems discussed in the preceding section is to guarantee the anonymity of agencies that submit use-of-force data to a national database. Virtually all national research studies on police use of force have guaranteed anonymity to law enforcement agencies in order to obtain their cooperation in providing data. Pate and Fridell included a letter with their survey instrument soliciting the cooperation of police executives and assuring them that, if they completed the questionnaire, their agencies would not be identified by name. In their final report, they state, "Despite these assurances, it is still possible that some agencies refused to participate or provided inaccurate or incomplete information."[44]

As discussed during the Police Use of Force Workshop, despite anonymity of response, police departments may still be identifiable through analysis of records in a data set. Large cities — New York, Los Angeles, and Chicago — stand out because their volume is so much greater than that of other cities. Even small cities can be identified if the records mention the State and the jurisdiction's population. Most workshop participants agreed that attempts at anonymity are unlikely to succeed since State or local law may require that such information must be made public or be released in response to an information request or subpoena.

---

[44]Pate and Fridell, p. 61.

Alternative approaches to data collection

Several approaches could be used in collecting data on police use of force. The selection depends largely on the definition of use of force and the purposes of the data collection. Early data collection efforts on force derived from field observations by trained sociologists. Their aim was to determine firsthand the circumstances under which police officers used force; they did not attempt to estimate the number of incidents or arrests in which force was actually applied. However, they were able to make insightful comments on the circumstances giving rise to force, the types of policies that departments should have on use of force, and the training that officers should receive. More recent studies have determined more precisely the types of force employed (verbal, handcuffs, batons, flashlights, firearms), the circumstances under which each was used (including force by the other party), and the volume of incidents or arrests in which force was applied.

As Kenneth Adams observes, these studies have depended on three general data sources: official records (from police and courts), surveys, and field observations. His breakdown is as follows:[45]

Official records

- Court records
- Citizen complaint records
- Arrest records
- Use-of-force records
- Injury records

Survey methods

- Surveys of police
- —Psychological tests
- —Self-report instruments
- —Peer nomination

- Citizen surveys
- —Victim surveys
- —Public opinion polls

These various approaches were a major topic of discussion at the Police Use of Force Workshop. Representatives from BJS presented several specific proposals on how national statistics on use of force

---

[45]Kenneth Adams, "Measuring the Prevalence of Police Abuse of Force," in *And Justice for All,* pp. 73-89.

could be acquired. The group reached no agreement on the most appropriate sources for national statistics. There was a general belief, however, that because no single source provided a complete and accurate picture, the Federal Government would need to obtain use-of-force data from several sources. The discussion provided insights that shaped the eventual decisions by NIJ and BJS to (1) replicate the Phoenix use-of-force study; (2) expand the BJS victimization study; and (3) provide initial grant funding for the establishment of a national database on police use of force from official police reports.

Official records

Court records

Court cases can be brought for excessive force through either criminal charges against the officers or civil claims against police and other jurisdictional officials. These cases may be filed in either Federal or State courts. Cases that go to trial result in a court decision on whether police used excessive force. In such cases, usable information would be available for data collection efforts. By contrast, for cases settled out of court, there may be no specific admission of guilt, and the litigants may agree not to disclose the terms of the settlement.

Only a small number of cases involving excessive force ever reach the courts.[46] In criminal matters, grand juries may be reluctant to indict the police. Civil cases are somewhat more likely to be litigated in court. Lawyers may represent a victim of excessive force on a contingency basis or receive fees during the preparation and litigation of a case regardless of the disposition. Further, the burden of proof in civil cases is lower than in criminal cases. However, civil cases are also subject to out-of-court settlement with restrictions about the outcome. Further complications are that lawyers handling civil cases may take only those

---

[46]For a fuller discussion on the utility of court cases, see Mary M. Cheh, "Are Law Suits an Answer to Police Brutality?" in *And Justice for All.*

with strong evidence and a potential for high settlements and that police officers may counterfile against the complainants.

In summary, court records offer detailed information about cases that result in trials with verdicts for or against the complainant. However, the picture of excessive force from such cases is limited because of the very small number of cases that result in official court action.

Citizen complaint records

Virtually all law enforcement agencies have procedures that allow citizens to lodge complaints against officers. Depending on department size and established policies, such complaints may be investigated by an internal review unit, designated commanders, an outside civilian review board, or a combination. The complaints may be sustained, unsustained, or unsubstantiated. In some cases, the complainant may decide to drop the allegations. Sustained complaints usually result in punishment or sanctions against the offending officers.

An important source of information about a variety of law enforcement issues, including policies and procedures on citizen complaints, is the Law Enforcement Management and Administrative Statistics (LEMAS) program administered by BJS. The LEMAS program began in 1987 with a nationwide survey of State and local law enforcement agencies, and was expanded in 1990 and 1993. The most recent LEMAS survey included data on whether the agency has a policy directive on citizen complaints, jurisdictional civilian complaint review board, person or group to whom the board reports, external review of complaints received, person with responsibility for making final disciplinary decision, and rights of officers or citizens to administrative appeal of the decision.[47] The LEMAS survey is not intended to collect statistics on the number of citizen complaints, but information from the tables can serve as a starting point for anyone interested in this subject.

A major difficulty in using citizen complaints as a gauge of excessive force is that a department's policies and procedures significantly influence the number and, perhaps, veracity of complaints received. Citizens may purposely or inadvertently be encouraged to make complaints or discouraged from making them. A department may choose not to make the complaint procedures well known to citizens, or it may encourage "informal" complaints to commanding officers before formal action. In addition, it is sometimes difficult for an arrested individual to seek

---

[47]Brian A Reaves and Pheny Z. Smith, *Law Enforcement Management and Administrative Statistics, 1993: Data for Individual State and Local Agencies with 100 or More Officers* (Washington: Bureau of Justice Statistics, 1995), Table 22a, p. 253. Also available under the BJS home page of the World Wide Web at *http://www.ojp.usdoj.gov/bjs/abstract/lemas93.htm.*

redress against the arresting officers, especially when the officers claim that he or she resisted arrest.

Researchers have noted obvious concerns about the proportion of complaints that are legitimate. Citizens may make frivolous complaints. Arrested persons may make complaints hoping that their charges will be reduced or dropped. Even when a complaint is investigated and seems plausible, it may be judged as unsustained by the police department because no third-party witnesses are available to support the complainant. In cases of the victim's word against the officer's word, the police department is likely to side with the officer.

The total number of uses of excessive force is no doubt underestimated by viewing citizen complaints. Before citizen complaints could be considered as a data source, an initial study of reporting procedures of police departments would have to be conducted.

Arrest records

Arrest records are an important source of data because arrestees are a high-risk population for being on the receiving end of force and excessive force by arresting officers. Moreover, arrest records contain details about arrestee characteristics (age, race, sex, etc.) and the circumstances of the arrest (charges, location, witnesses, etc.) that may be unavailable from other sources.

The disadvantage is that many incidents that involve use of force by officers do not result in an arrest. Even when an arrest is made, officers may not report whether force was employed. The arrest report form may not request information on the use of force, or the arresting officer may decide not to include the information. The picture is further complicated when officers include charges of resisting arrest. Officers may improperly include such charges to protect themselves when they believe they have used excessive force. These considerations have led some researchers to propose the tallying of resisting arrest charges as still another component of a *composite* index of the prevalence of questionable police-civilian interaction, even though such charges would be too imprecise an index in the absence of other indicators.

Arrest records may be of greater utility at the local level than as national indicators of force. Officers who use force frequently or who use excessive force are often the highest producers of arrests in a department. They may simply be more aggressive in making arrests than other officers. Arrest records can be analyzed as an early warning system of officers prone to use excessive force. However, the arrest records must be analyzed carefully because these officers may simply have more opportunities to make arrests, and therefore more opportunities to use force.

Use-of-force reports

As reported by Geller and Scott (1992) and Pate and
Fridell (1993), almost all police departments require
a report when an officer uses deadly force. Reporting
other uses of force, however, is not always mandatory
in departments. Pate and Fridell report that —
95% of their responding departments require reports
for use of deadly force,
82% for batons,
72% for chemical agents, and
only 29% for handcuffs.[48]

There may be a trend nationwide for police departments to improve reporting procedures on all uses of
force. The efforts of SACOP under the IACP indicate
renewed interest in obtaining more information about
use-of-force incidents. As indicated elsewhere in this
report, law enforcement officials believe those records
will show how infrequently excessive force occurs
and that the great majority of arrests and incidents are
handled by police without turning to force.

The national database on police use of force that will
be established under the auspices of the IACP offers
an opportunity for researchers to obtain national
statistics based on data reported by local police departments. The advantage of the IACP's effort is the
potential for standardization of reports and a high rate

---

[48]Pate and Fridell, pp. 65 and 69.

of participation by police departments. However, those goals are not expected to be achieved for many years.

Injury records

Virtually all police departments maintain reports of injuries to citizens and police. For police employees, reports cover injuries from arrests, automobile accidents, workplace accidents, and many other sources. For citizens, reports cover injuries from automobile accidents, arrests, and other incidents.

Injury reports are a potential source of information on the most serious uses of force by police, but they obviously do not include all uses of force. Chemical agents (such as pepper spray), pushing, and handcuffs seldom cause sufficient injury to warrant a report. As a national measure, injury reports would therefore tell only part of the story, but they could be useful in tandem with other sources.

In sum, under current reporting procedures, official records from courts and police underestimate the incidence of police use of force and excessive force. Only a small proportion of incidents ever reach court proceedings. People who are the subjects of police force do not always make official complaints to police, and when they do, their complaints are not always substantiated. Arrests frequently include use of force, but are again only a portion of the circumstances under

which police use force. Departmental use-of-force reports are not mandatory for many types of force, and
injury records maintained by police departments
reflect only the most serious incidents of force.

For a national picture of police use of force, the most
promising approach with official records is improved
reporting by police departments. The incentives for a
local police department are many, as better reporting
would —

• show the public that the police department wants
to control its use of force

• help the department establish better training
programs

• serve as an early warning system about officers
prone to excessive use of force or use of excessive
force

• serve as an early warning system about systemic
problems that needlessly put officers in untenable
situations where they are criticized if they do and
criticized if they do not use coercive force.

Surveys of police

Adams describes three approaches for obtaining information about use of force through surveys of police: psychological tests of police, self-report instruments, and peer nomination.

Many police departments employ psychological tests during the hiring process as a screening mechanism. Their use with current employees is less prevalent. The key point about psychological tests is that they measure the *potential* for violence, rather than actual incidence of violence. The reliability of these tests to identify violence potential has been questioned.[49]

Another approach is simply to ask police officers about their use of force. Under a study funded by BJS, the Illinois Criminal Justice Information Authority surveyed police officers in Illinois (not including Chicago) on a variety of issues relating to police ethics.[50] They received 861 completed surveys from officers. With regard to the questions about use of force, 21.1% said that in the last year they had seen an officer use more force than was necessary to appre-

---

[49]J. Douglas Grant and Joan Grant, "Officer Selection and the Prevention of Abuse of Force," in *And Justice for All*.
[50]Christine Martin, Peter B. Bensinger, and Thomas F. Baker, Illinois Municipal Officers' Perceptions of Police Ethics (Chicago: Illinois Criminal Justice Information Authority, 1994). The Chicago Police Department did not participate in the study after the Chicago Fraternal Order of Police decided not to endorse the project.

hend a suspect, 5.7% said they had seen an officer cover up excessive force, and 8.5% reported knowledge of an officer failing to report excessive force. It should be noted that these statistics do not translate into the rate of abuses per officer or the incidence of excessive force per arrest.

A final approach — peer nomination — is to ask officers to identify other officers who are prone to using force. Researchers have used this approach in the past to identify positive characteristics, such as excellence at solving problems, resolving conflicts, or conducting investigations. It is open to question whether officers would identify officers with negative characteristics.[51]

In summary, surveys of police officers probably have no role in developing a national picture of police use of force or excessive force. Their use is limited to the local level, where such surveys may identify potential "bad apples" among police applicants or current officers or, if the approach in Charlotte with peer reviews is successful, may identify good police work and ways to attain desired improvements.

---

[51]At the request of Chief Dennis Nowicki, Charlotte-Mecklenburg (North Carolina) Police Department, Mr. William Geller of the Police Executive Research Forum is currently assisting the department in developing a panel of officers' peers to conduct a "tactical debriefing" of police use of force with the involved officers. The panel's work will not trigger any disciplinary process, but instead is for the purpose of applying seasoned street officers' experience to gain further insight into police use of force.

Surveys of citizens

Two approaches to citizen surveys are public opinion polls and victimization surveys. Public opinion polls, such as the familiar Gallup polls, are a relatively fast and cost-effective way to obtain national estimates on a variety of issues. In a Gallup poll conducted in March 1991, respondents were asked, "Have you ever been physically mistreated or abused by the police?" The poll yielded the following results:

• Five percent of all respondents said they had been physically mistreated or abused by the police.

• Nine percent of non-whites answered in the affirmative to the question of physical mistreatment or abuse by the police.

• Twenty percent of respondents said they knew someone who had been physically mistreated or abused by the police.

Considerable care must be taken in conducting any citizen poll to ensure that accurate information is obtained. For example, respondents may have interpreted "mistreated or abused" in several ways, ranging from a slight push to a severe beating. The results may underestimate the incidence of police force if respondents had only violent confrontations in mind. A national sample of citizens must be carefully selected so that the group of respondents reflects the general population. National polling groups have become especially adept in their sampling procedures. Finally, many polls suffer from the inability of respondents to recollect history in the correct time frame. A typical error is for a respondent to bring an incident forward in time indicating, for example, that something happened in the last year when, in fact, it happened 18 months ago.

The expansion of the national victimization survey to include questions about police use of force has already been mentioned and will be described in more detail in the next section. The victimization survey offers several possibilities for developing more reliable estimates on the incidence of police use of force. Notably, BJS has developed statistical procedures for weighting the results to obtain national estimates of crime victimization. The results for police use of force may also be valuable for comparisons against other sources, including official reports of force.

National data collection efforts

In response to the mandate of the 1994 Crime Act, two national data collection efforts have begun to collect data on police use of force. BJS will expand its annual victimization study to include questions about whether respondents have experienced use of force by police. The IACP has been awarded a grant by BJS and NIJ for the first phase of a four-phase effort to establish a national database containing information from police departments on their incidence of force. The following sections discuss each of those efforts.

Victimization study

BJS will develop a police-public contact supplement to the National Crime Victimization Survey (NCVS), the second largest ongoing household survey sponsored by the Federal Government. This will be used to estimate the extent of public exposure to the use of force by law enforcement officers. The NCVS maintains semiannual contact with a nationally representative sample of more than 100,000 persons residing in about 50,000 households in order to learn about crime and its consequences on citizens.

In 1995, BJS took steps toward developing a police-public contact survey to ask questions about the use of both appropriate and inappropriate force during police-public encounters. In coordination with NIJ, BJS commissioned several experts to prepare discussion papers on alternative measurement issues associated with the use of force and convened a national panel, composed of representatives of law enforcement and those with an interest in the quality of law enforcement services, to consider the range of statistical opportunities for carrying out the mandates in Section 210402 of the 1994 Crime Act.

During 1996, BJS expects to pretest the police-public contact survey within the NCVS. The pretest will help BJS determine the types of questions likely to ensure systematic, national, long-term collection of information on the incidence, prevalence, characteristics, and official responses to excessive force.

The pretest questions will cover the following major subjects:

• Types of police-citizen encounters during a 12-month reference period

• Whether force was used

• Any provocation by the respondent preceding police use of force

• Demographic characteristics of respondents and law enforcement officers perceived to have been involved in use-of-force incidents

• Injuries sustained by respondents and law enforcement officers as a result of use of force

• Actions initiated by respondents to protest the use of force in the incident.

Attaching items about the use of force to an existing national survey is a simplified and less costly alternative to gathering available information directly from law enforcement agencies. Given the enormous variability in law enforcement agency practices with respect to maintaining data on use-of-force events, the NCVS affords much greater control over the comparability and timeliness of collected information.

Section 210402 of the 1994 Crime Act does not specify what data the Attorney General must collect and report annually on excessive force by law enforcement officers. As a result, there is wide latitude in the kinds of information that could be reported.

Current plans call for the pretest questionnaire to be fielded in late spring of 1996, after a period of public review through the Federal Register and OMB review under the Paperwork Reduction Act. As with the NCVS, the Bureau of the Census will serve as the collection agent for BJS. BJS plans to conduct a 3- to 4-month pretest of approximately 10,000 to 12,000 individuals. If the pretest suggests that the NCVS could be a useful method, among others, for collecting information on police use of force, then funds could be sought from the Administration and the Congress to support such an enhancement.

IACP study[52]

Based on the success of the VACOP effort, the IACP has received grant funding for Phase I of a long-term program to create a comprehensive Police Use of Force Database. The database will contain information provided by police departments on use-of-force incidents. The four phases of the program are these:

- Phase I: Expansion of the VACOP approach to five additional States

- Phase II: Detailed analysis of Phase I data and expansion to additional States

- Phase III: Development of annual reports

- Phase IV: Promotion of secondary data analysis

Funding has been provided for the first phase as a 12-month effort consisting of two major tasks:
(1) building law enforcement consensus on the need for a national database, and
(2) structuring local data collection efforts in Virginia and five other States.
Under the supervision of its research director, the IACP has established a National Use of Force Database Center for accomplishing all grant activities.

---

[52]The information in this section is summarized from *National Police Use of Force Database Project: An IACP Proposal* (Alexandria, Virginia: International Association of Chiefs of Police, September 1995), approved by BJS and NIJ in September 1995.

Phase I includes a project advisory committee that will provide advice on what data should be collected from police departments and how the data should be collected. The advisory committee will include members from BJS, NIJ, the IACP Executive Committee, the IACP's State Associations of Chiefs of Police (SACOP) Division, State associations of chiefs of police from the six selected States, the IACP's State and Provincial Directorate, the academic community, the National Law Enforcement Technology Center, and the National Sheriffs' Association.

The consensus-building task of Phase I will include the following key activities:

• Identify six pilot States (including Virginia) for implementation of the national database design.[53]

• Develop an endorsement by the IACP Executive Committee to support the need for the national database.

• Publish an article in *The Police Chief* about the project and its benefits to law enforcement.

• Train selected State SACOP representatives to serve as "data advisors."

• Publish additional information in selected State association periodicals.

---

[53] Initial candidates for the pilot States are Virginia, Vermont, New York, Arkansas, Washington, and New Jersey.

The second task in Phase I includes revising the data elements based on the VACOP model, changing the data collection software as necessary, providing training and technical assistance in each pilot State, preparing a data collection manual, and disseminating the data collection package to law enforcement agencies in each pilot State. It is expected that these activities will be completed by the end of the Phase I effort.

The timetable and level of effort for the remaining phases will depend on Phase I experiences. However, several key features of the latter phases are important for the long-term success of the IACP's national database. Phase II includes an assessment of the success of data collection efforts in the six pilot States, including the amount, representativeness, quality, and reliability of data collected. After completing the assessment, the IACP will target groups of five new states incrementally until a comprehensive national database is in place. The expansion will be a multi-year effort with continual assessment and updating.

The IACP, through its National Use of Force Database Center, will serve as the repository of all State-level data. It will prepare annual reports for national consumption. The first report will be based on the six States in the pilot test, with subsequent reports based on additional States as they join the national effort.

Finally, the last phase is to encourage additional analysis of the aggregate data available from the center to determine national trends in police use of force. In the 1920s, the IACP tried nobly but ultimately without success to launch a pioneering national crime reporting system. Eventually the task was transferred to the FBI and became what we know of today as the Uniform Crime Reporting System.[54] It is hoped that in the 1990s and on this sensitive subject, the IACP will have a more productive experience enrolling the support of its constituents.

---

[54]William A. Geller and Norval Morris, "Relations between Federal and Local Police," in *Modern Policing,* edited by Michael Tonry and Norval Morris (Chicago: University of Chicago Press, 1992, pp. 231-348).

Conclusions

For decades, criminal justice experts have been calling
for increased collection of data on police use of force.
Section 210402 of the 1994 Crime Act now requires
the Attorney General to acquire data about the use
of excessive force by law enforcement officers.

BJS and NIJ will continue to work with police organizations, researchers, and citizens to establish accurate
and reliable databases on police use of force. Clearly,
this will require both standard definitions and uniform
data sources. As described in the *Foreword* and other
sections of this publication, BJS and NIJ are currently
sponsoring several field tests, pilot projects, and surveys to achieve these ends.

References

Adams, Kenneth. "Measuring the Prevalence of Police Abuse of Force." *In And Justice for All: Understanding and Controlling Police Abuse of Force, edited by William A. Geller and Hans Toch, 61-97. Washington, D.C.: Police Executive Research Forum, 1995.

Alpert, Geoffrey P., and Lorie A. Fridell. Police Vehicles and Firearms: Instruments of Deadly Force. Prospect Heights, Illinois: Waveland Press, Inc., 1992.

Alpert, Geoffrey P., and William C. Smith. "How Reasonable Is the Reasonable Man?: Police and Excessive Force," *The Journal of Criminal Law and Criminology,* 85(2) 1994, 481-501.

Bittner, Egon. *The Functions of Police in Modern Society.* Washington: National Institute of Mental Health, 1970.

Cheh, Mary M. "Are Law Suits an Answer to Police Brutality?" In *And Justice for All: Understanding and Controlling Police Abuse of Force,* edited by William A. Geller and Hans Toch, 233-259. Washington: Police Executive Research Forum, 1995.

Condon, Richard J. *Police Use of Deadly Force in New York State.* Albany, New York: Division of Criminal Justice Services, 1985.

Cox, Terry C., Jerry S. Faughn, and William M. Nixon. "Police Use of Metal Flashlights as Weapons: An Analysis of Relevant Problems," *Journal of Police Science and Administration*, 13(3) 1985: 244-50.

DeVesa, Frederick P. *Report of the Attorney General's Task Force on the Use of Force in Law Enforcement.* Trenton, New Jersey: 1992.

Federal Bureau of Investigation. *Volume 1: Data Collection Guidelines, National Incident-Based Reporting System.* Washington, D.C.: Federal Bureau of Investigation, 1988.

Federal Bureau of Investigation. *Crime in the United States, Uniform Crime Reports for the United States, 1994.* Washington, D.C.: Federal Bureau of Investigation, 1995.

Friedrich, Robert J. "Police Use of Force: Individuals, Situations, and Organizations," *Annals of the American Academy of Political and Social Science,* 452(November 1980): 82-97.

Fyfe, James J. "Police Use of Deadly Force: Research and Reform," *Justice Quarterly,* 5(2) 1988: 165-201.

Garner, Joel H., and John Buchanan. *Executive Summary: Understanding the Use of Force by and Against the Police.* Washington, D.C.: National Institute of Justice, 1995.

Geller, William A. "Officer Restraint in the Use of Deadly Force: The Next Frontier in Police Shooting Research," *Journal of Police Science and Administration,* 10(2) 1985: 151-77.

Geller, William A., and Kevin J. Karales. *Split-Second Decisions: Shootings of and by Chicago Police.* Chicago, Illinois: Chicago Law Enforcement Study Group, 1981.

Geller, William A., and Norval Morris. "Relations Between Federal and Local Police." In *Modern Policing,* edited by Michael Tonry and Norval Morris, 231-348. Chicago, Illinois: University of Chicago Press, 1992.

Geller, William A., and Michael Scott. *Deadly Force: What We Know: A Practitioner's Desk Reference to Police-Involved Shootings.* Washington, D.C.: Police Executive Research Forum, 1992.

Geller, William A., and Hans Toch, eds. *And Justice for All: Understanding and Controlling Police Abuse of Force.* Washington, D.C.: Police Executive Research Forum, 1995.

Geller, William A., and Hans Toch. "Improving Our Understanding and Control of Police Abuse of Force: Recommendations for Research and Action. " In *And Justice for All: Understanding and Controlling Police Abuse of Force,* edited by William A. Geller and Hans Toch, 277-337. Washington, D.C.: Police Executive Research Forum, 1995.

Grant, J. Douglas, and Joan Grant. "Officer Selection and the Prevention of Abuse of Force," in *And Justice for All: Understanding and Controlling Police Abuse of Force,* edited by William A. Geller and Hans Toch, 151-162. Washington, D.C.: Police Executive Research Forum, 1995

Klockars, Carl B. "A Theory of Excessive Force and Its Control." In *And Justice for All: Understanding and Controlling Police Abuse of Force,* edited by William A. Geller and Hans Toch, 11-69. Washington, D.C.: Police Executive Research Forum, 1995.

Martin, Christine, Peter B. Bensinger, and Thomas F. Baker. *Illinois Municipal Officers' Perceptions of Police Ethics.* Chicago, Illinois: Illinois Criminal Justice Information Authority, 1994.

Matulia, Kenneth J. *A Balance of Forces.* Gaithersburg, Maryland: International Association of Chiefs of Police, 1982.

McEwen, Tom, and Frank Leahy. *Final Report: Less Than Lethal Force Technologies in Law Enforcement and Correctional Agencies.* Washington, D.C.: National Institute of Justice, 1994.

Miller, Neal. "Less-Than-Lethal Force Weaponry: Law Enforcement and Correctional Agency Civil Law Liability for the Use of Excessive Force," *Creighton Law Review,* 28(3) 1995: 733-94.

Milton, Catherine H., Jeanne Wahl Halleck, James
     Lardner, and Gary L. Abrecht. *Police Use
     of Deadly Force.* Washington, D.C.: Police
     Foundation, 1977.

Pate, Antony M., and Lorie A. Fridell. *Police Use
     of Force: Official Reports, Citizen Complaints,
     and Legal Consequences.* Washington, D.C.:
     Police Foundation, 1993.

Reaves, Brian A., and Pheny Z. Smith. *Law Enforce-
     ment Management and Administrative Statistics,
     1993: Data for Individual State and Local
     Agencies with 100 or More Officers.*
     Washington, D.C.: Bureau of Justice Statistics,
     1995.

Reiss, Albert J., Jr. *The Police and The Public.*
     New Haven, Connecticut: Yale University Press,
     1971.

Sherman, Lawrence W., and Robert H. Langworthy.
     "Measuring Homicide by Police Officers," *The
     Journal of Criminal Law and Criminology,* 70(4)
     1979: 546-560.

Skolnick, Jerome H., and James J. Fyfe. *Above the
     Law: Police and the Excessive Use of Force.*
     New York: The Free Press, 1993.

Tonry, Michael, and Norval Morris, eds. *Modern
     Policing.* Chicago, Illinois: University of
     Chicago Press, 1992.

Virginia Association of Chiefs of Police. *1994 Use
     of Force Report.* November 1994.

Worden, Robert E. "The 'Causes' of Police Brutality: Theory and Evidence on Police Use of Force." In *And Justice for All: Understanding and Controlling Police Abuse of Force,* edited by William A. Geller and Hans Toch, 31-60. Washington, D.C.: Police Executive Research Forum, 1995.

Public databases

Bureau of Justice Statistics. *Law Enforcement Management and Administrative Statistics, 1990.* Inter-University Consortium for Political and Social Research (ICPSR), University of Michigan. Database ICPSR 9749.

Garner, Joel, and John Buchanan. *Understanding the Use of Force By and Against the Police.* Inter-University Consortium for Political and Social Research (ICPSR), University of Michigan. Database forthcoming.

Matulia, Kenneth J. *Police Use of Deadly Force, 1970-1979.* Inter-University Consortium for Political and Social Research (ICPSR), University of Michigan. Database ICPSR 9018.

Ostrom, Elinor, Roger B. Parks, and Gordon Whitaker. *Police Services Study, Phase II, 1977: Rochester, St. Louis, and St. Petersburgh.* Inter-University Consortium for Political and Social Research (ICPSR), University of Michigan. Database ICPSR 8605.

Pate, Antony M., and Lorie E. Fridell. *Police Use of Force: Official Reports, Citizen Complaints, and Legal Consequences, 1991-1992.* Inter-University Consortium for Political and Social Research (ICPSR), University of Michigan. Database ICPSR 6274.

Reiss, Albert J., Jr. *Patterns of Behavior in Police and Citizen Transactions: Boston, Chicago, and Washington, DC, 1966.* Inter-University Consortium for Political and Social Research (ICPSR), University of Michigan. Database ICPSR 9086.

Appendix

Attendee List for May 31, 1995
Police Use of Force Workshop

Yoshio Akiyama
Uniform Crime Reporting Program
Federal Bureau of Investigation
U.S. Department of Justice
Washington, DC

Geoffrey P. Alpert
Professor
School of Criminal Justice
University of South Carolina
Columbia, SC

Tom Arnold
Deputy Director
Metro-Dade Police Department
Miami, FL

Ronald Banks
Assistant Chief
Los Angeles Police Department
Los Angeles, CA

Peter Bobinski
Acting Unit Chief
Civil Rights Unit, C.I.D.
FBI
U.S. Department of Justice
Washington, DC

John L. Buchanan
Captain
Phoenix Police Department
Phoenix, AZ

Donald Cahill
Chairman
National Legislative Committee
Fraternal Order of Police
Washington, DC

Jan M. Chaiken
Director
Bureau of Justice Statistics
U.S. Department of Justice
Washington, DC

Bennie Click
Chief of Police
Dallas Police Department
Dallas, TX

Jay Cochran, Jr.
Executive Director
Virginia Association of Chiefs of Police
Richmond, VA

Karla Dobinski
Deputy Chief, Civil Rights Division
Criminal Section, U.S. Department of Justice
Washington, DC

Steven Edwards
Community Oriented Policing
U.S. Department of Justice
Washington, DC

Dora Falls
Lieutenant
Dallas Police Department
Dallas, TX

John R. Firman
Director of Research
International Association of Chiefs of Police
Alexandria, VA

Lorie Fridell
Assistant Professor
School of Criminology and Criminal Justice
Florida State University
Tallahassee, FL

James J. Fyfe
Professor
Department of Criminal Justice
Temple University
Philadelphia, PA

Saunji Fyffe
Budget Officer
National Institute of Justice
U.S. Department of Justice
Washington, DC

Joel Garner
School of Criminal Justice
Rutgers University
Washington, DC

William A. Geller
Associate Director
Police Executive Research Forum
Wilmette, IL

Jack Greene
Professor
Department of Criminal Justice
Temple University
Philadelphia, PA

Larry Greenfeld
Deputy Director
Bureau of Justice Statistics
U.S. Department of Justice
Washington, DC

Edwin E. Hamilton
Research Analyst
Police Foundation
Washington, DC

Ira Harris
Executive Director
National Organization of Black Law
  Enforcement Executives
Alexandria, VA

William Johnson
General Counsel
National Association of Police Organizations
Washington, DC

Randall K. Kocsis
Uniform Crime Reporting Program
FBI
U.S. Department of Justice
Washington, DC

Robert Langworthy
Program Manager
Office of Research and Evaluation
National Institute of Justice
U.S. Department of Justice
Washington, DC

Mark Masling
Senior Trial Attorney
Civil Rights Division
Special Litigation Section
U.S. Department of Justice
Washington, DC

William Matthews
Deputy Director, Administration
Police Foundation
Washington, DC

Lois Mock
Program Manager
National Institute of Justice
U.S. Department of Justice
Washington, DC

Robert Moossy
Trial Attorney
Civil Rights Division
Special Litigation Section
U.S. Department of Justice
Washington, DC

Eric Nordstrom
Intern
National Institute of Justice
U.S. Department of Justice
Washington, DC

Dennis E. Nowicki
Chief of Police
Law Enforcement Center
Charlotte-Mecklenburg Police Department
Charlotte, NC

Antony M. Pate
Assistant Professor
School of Criminology and Criminal Justice
Florida State University
Tallahassee, FL

Carol Petrie
Director, Planning and Management
National Institute of Justice
U.S. Department of Justice
Washington, DC

James W. Powers
Chief of Police
Fredericksburg Police Department
Fredericksburg, VA

Brian Reaves
Chief, Law Enforcement Statistics Unit
Bureau of Justice Statistics
U.S. Department of Justice
Washington, DC

Winifred Reed
Social Science Program Manager
Crime Control Division
National Institute of Justice
U.S. Department of Justice
Washington, DC

Elsie L. Scott
Deputy Commissioner of Training
Police Academy
New York City Police Department
New York, NY

Ellen Scrivner
Director
Grant Monitoring Division
Community Oriented Policing Services
Washington, DC

Michael E. Smith
President
Vera Institute of Justice, Inc.
New York, NY

Steve Smith
Chief, Law Enforcement and Adjudication Unit
Bureau of Justice Statistics
U.S. Department of Justice
Washington, DC

Hector Soto
Executive Director, New York City
Civilian Complaint Review Board
New York, NY

Ronald Sylve
Leutenant
Internal Investigation Division
Seattle Police Department
Seattle, WA

Dianne Thompson
Program Analyst
Civil Rights Division
Criminal Section
U.S. Department of Justice
Washington, DC

Jeremy Travis
Director
National Institute of Justice
U.S. Department of Justice
Washington, DC

Peggy Triplett
Chief Executive Officer
Triplett Associates
Public Administration Service
Washington, DC

Larry Vardell
Chief of Police
Williamsburg Police Department
Williamsburg, VA

Christy Visher
Science Advisor to the Director
National Institute of Justice
U.S. Department of Justice
Washington, DC

Chriss Wetherington
Special Assistant
National Institute of Justice
U.S. Department of Justice
Washington, DC

www.ingramcontent.com/pod-product-compliance
Lightning Source LLC
Chambersburg PA
CBHW060635290526
45793CB00001B/259